FAIRIES
101

ALSO BY DOREEN VIRTUE

All of the above are available at your local bookstore,
or may be ordered by visiting:

Hay House USA: **www.hayhouse.com**®
Hay House Australia: **www.hayhouse.com.au**
Hay House UK: **www.hayhouse.co.uk**
Hay House South Africa: **www.hayhouse.co.za**
Hay House India: **www.hayhouse.co.in**

Doreen's Website: **www.AngelTherapy.com**

FAIRIES 101

An Introduction to Connecting,
Working, and Healing with the Fairies
and Other Elementals

DOREEN VIRTUE

HAY HOUSE, INC.
Carlsbad, California • New York City
London • Sydney • Johannesburg
Vancouver • Hong Kong • New Delhi

Published and distributed in the United States by: Hay House, Inc.:
www.hayhouse.com • *Published and distributed in Australia by:* Hay
House Australia Pty. Ltd.: www.hayhouse.com.au • *Published and distributed in the United Kingdom by:* Hay House UK, Ltd.: www.hay
house.co.uk • *Published and distributed in the Republic of South Africa by:* Hay House SA (Pty), Ltd.: www.hayhouse.co.za • *Distributed
in Canada by:* Raincoast: www.raincoast.com • *Published in India by:*
Publishers India: www.hayhouse.co.in

Editorial supervision: Jill Kramer • *Design:* Amy Rose Grigoriou

Illustrations: © 2001–2006 Howard David Johnson;
www.howarddavidjohnson.com
The Green Man illustration, page 77: © Wendy Andrews

Library of Congress Cataloging-in-Publication Data

Virtue, Doreen.
  Fairies 101 : an introduction to connecting, working, and healing
with the fairies and other elementals / Doreen Virtue.
     p. cm.
  ISBN-13: 978-1-4019-0760-0 (hardcover) 1. Fairies. I. Title. II. Title:
Fairies one hundred one. III. Title: Fairies one hundred and one.
  BF1552.V565 2007
  133.1'4--dc22

                          2006012439

            Tradepaper ISBN: 978-1-4019-3183-4
               Digital ISBN: 978-1-4019-2985-5

            14 13 12 11   6 5 4 3

               1st edition, March 2007
               3rd edition, July 2011

                  Printed in China

CONTENTS

Introduction

"I *DO* BELIEVE IN FAIRIES . . . I DO, I DO, I DO!"

*I*f you believe in fairies, you're not alone. In my global travels, I meet people worldwide who tell me about their encounters with the magical fairy realms. They fondly recall childhood experiences of connecting with fairies, and some continue to talk with these beings as adults. (Most of them whisper this information to me.)

I know that *I* believe in fairies . . . do you? As a little girl, I spent many hours staring at paintings of fairies with feelings of recognition and familiarity. Although I saw angels and deceased people as a child, I didn't see my first fairy until adulthood. Since then, I've developed a benevolent and

vii

loving relationship with these beings. I have enormous respect for their mission of healing the environment, protecting animals, and reminding us of the importance of play.

Although surveys show that the majority of people believe that angels are real, fewer believe in fairies. In many bookstores, angels have their own shelf, while books about fairies are relegated to the "mythology" section. Perhaps this is because fairies, unlike angels, only make themselves known to those who believe.

I've found that people in the United Kingdom and Australia believe in fairies more than those in other countries do. These are also the places where I find the largest populations of fairies. So are there more fairies because people believe in them? Or do people believe in them because there are more fairies?

Other pockets of strong fairy connections include upstate New York; Hawaii; Iceland; and Ontario, Canada. In fact, I receive more fairy stories from readers living in Ontario than any other geographical location!

Those who believe in fairies receive wonderful assistance, as you'll read about in this book. Fairies help us manifest our earthly needs such as buying, renting, or selling a home. They also bring us jobs and money. Fairies help our gardens and pets in amazing ways, and they're especially happy to help anyone who shares their concern and love for the environment and animals.

Angels and fairies are both God's creations with important missions, and they help humans in vital ways. Archangels and guardian angels help us with our spiritual path and provide protection. Fairies are the guardians of nature and animals.

The more people who believe in fairies, the more power they have. This power allows them to clean the earth, air, and waters.

Please join me in affirming the immortal words of Peter Pan: "I *do* believe in fairies . . . I do, I do, I do!" These words brought Tinkerbell back to life, and they can also give more life and energy to fairies everywhere.

— **Doreen Virtue**

Chapter One

WHO ARE THE FAIRIES?

*"Every blade of grass has an angel
bending over it saying, 'Grow! Grow!'"*

— The Talmud (ancient Jewish text)

The angels that the Talmud refers to are the "nature angels." Each of them has a special assignment, and nature angels oversee the environment and animals. Because nature is composed of basic elements such as earth, water, air, and fire, nature angels are from the "elemental realm." There are several different types of elementals, who vary according to the task they specialize in. The elementals that we'll focus on in this book are the fairies.

Fairies are angels who reside very close to the earth so that they can perform their Divine mission of protecting nature and animals. Some fairies have wings like dragonflies, while others have butterfly-like wings in contrast to the feathered bird wings of guardian and archangels.

Unlike guardian and archangels, fairies have egos. In this way, they're similar to humans in that they make judgments. When fairies meet you, they judge you for how you treat the environment and animals.

Fairies don't expect anyone to be perfect. However, if you do your best to recycle, use nontoxic cleaning supplies, are kind to animals, and such, then fairies will give you their high regard and grant you favors. If the fairies judge that you're unkind to the environment or animals, they may play tricks on you. This is why they have mischievous reputations.

Fairies are sometimes called "faeries" or "fae." Yet no matter what you call them or how you spell their names, the fairies genuinely want to help you live a healthier, happier, and more prosperous life. Because they're so close to the earth, the fairies can assist you with material concerns involving money, home, health, your gardens, and your pets.

≈≈

Did you see fairies as a child? Many children do. The fairies are more likely to reveal themselves to open-minded and pure-hearted kids than to adults (unless the man's or woman's heart is open and pure as well). Fairies also love to help children in many ways, as you'll read about in this book.

Fairies remind us to lighten up, play, and enjoy life more often. They love parties, music, and dance. They also love rich sweets, and some elementals have been known to drink alcohol. Yet in spite of their mirth, they still get their responsibilities met—which is one of their lessons to all of us.

The fairies remind us that:

- Life is joyful and fun.

- Nature needs and deserves our respect.

- Animals are our brothers and sisters.

- Everything is alive.

- Play is very important.

- You can magically manifest everything you need (especially with their help).

Chapter Two

HOUSES, CAREERS, AND OTHER GIFTS FROM THE FAIRIES

To connect with the fairies, go outdoors. This is where they live. The fairies love flowers, trees, shrubs, and bodies of water. They love gardens that grow freely, without tight manicuring or pesticides. As you'll read within these pages, the fairies can help you with your garden so that you don't need to use chemicals!

Once you're outside, tell the fairies that you'd like to meet them. You can do this silently, aloud, or by leaving an offering. The fairies hear your thoughts, and they love gifts. They're especially fond of candy (unwrapped, of course) and shiny objects like crystals.

The fairies will scan you to get a sense of how well you treat the environment and animals. If you pass this test, they'll give you an assignment that you'll receive as a thought or feeling. Usually, the fairies will ask you to gather and dispose of trash from the area you're standing in. If you do so, they will gladly help you with whatever you ask, as Lisa Grubb discovered:

Lisa was upset by the all the trash that littered her favorite campsite. She'd just arrived to enjoy a camping trip and was in the process of gathering firewood. Yet instead of finding wood, all she could see was rubbish covering the grounds.

So Lisa started cleaning up the mountainside. With each piece of trash she picked up, she blessed the land and forgave the people who'd littered. She gathered six large bags of rubbish, but still had no firewood for her campsite. There weren't even any burned-out logs in the camp fire pits.

Lisa decided to drive to a nearby facility to buy some wood. So she gathered her bags of rubbish and headed down the mountain. She put the rubbish in containers but found that no one was available to sell her some firewood.

She returned to her campsite and figured that she'd find wood later or just bundle up for the night. As she neared her campsite, Lisa was amazed to find a large stack of wood that was cut, split, and neatly stacked. She'd only been gone for 15 minutes and no one else was around. Where could the wood have come from?

All throughout the week, no one came to claim the wood. That's when Lisa knew for sure that fairies had provided for her wonderful retreat that week, and rewarded her for her thoughtful conservation efforts.

I spoke with Lisa after she submitted this story to me, and discovered that she's been talking to the fairies since she was a little girl. She is very ecology conscious and does what she can to help the environment. She says that the fairies always help her in exchange for her kindness to nature.

Like Lisa, Priscilla Palmer was rewarded by the fairies for picking up trash. The fairies' gifts usually consist of items made from Mother Earth, like Lisa's firewood and Priscilla's crystal:

As Priscilla walked along the shores of Laguna Beach, California, she noticed a cove littered with empty water bottles, fast-food containers, cigarette butts, Styrofoam cups, and other plastic. She heard the fairies implore her to pick up the trash. Not having any bag to put the trash into, Priscilla promised to pick it up later.

As much as she wanted to keep her promise, the thought of picking up trash and touching someone else's germs disgusted her. The next day in meditation, she heard the fairies say, "You promised to pick up the trash at Moss Cove. Are you going to do it?" Before she had a chance to argue with herself or the fairies, she grabbed some trash bags and returned to the cove.

Priscilla picked up all the trash that was easily accessible. Then her eye was drawn to an empty water bottle up on the hillside. She had to balance herself precariously to reach it. Upon picking up the bottle, she found a beautiful natural quartz crystal beneath it! Here was a gift from the fairies for keeping her promise!

As Priscilla picked up the crystal, she could feel the healing ocean and earth energy within it. She held it to her heart and thanked the fairies for their kindness. She heard them say, "Thank *you* for your kindness!"

So fairies offer unsolicited gifts to show us their gratitude for taking care of Mother Earth. Yet, if you're regularly showing respect toward the environment and animals, the fairies will help you whenever you ask. You don't need to do environmental work immediately before you ask the fairies for a gift. They'll help whenever you ask, provided that you do something nice for the planet on a regular basis.

Fairies are brilliant manifestors, meaning that they know how to attract or create dreams and make them a reality. They remind us of the importance of staying true and positive about our desires.

Lisa Center received lots of help from the fairies in turning her life around in a positive way. She had been unemployed and renting a room at a friend's house, while her children lived apart from her. Lisa desperately wanted to live with her kids in her own home by Christmastime. She also wished to get away from her traditional social-worker career and be employed in alternative healing.

Lisa recalls, "I spent as much time as possible outdoors and searched for work daily. I dreamed of living with my kids again. I'd visualize us spending Christmas in my home, decorated as if it were Santa's cottage."

One morning during meditation, Lisa was guided to find a piece of construction paper. She selected a piece of pink paper and began sketching without any plans for what she'd draw. She said, "I could hear gentle whispering in my ears as I drew, saying, 'No, longer hair. No, draw the ears more like this. Yes, that's it.'"

Finally, Lisa asked what she was drawing. The voice answered, "Not what. Whom!" So Lisa asked *whom* she was drawing. The voice replied, "Lilitte. I am the fairy who will be helping you manifest your dreams. I am with you, and you can call upon me for help at any time."

Every time Lisa would lose faith in her search for employment, she'd look at the pink paper with Lilitte's portrait and ask her for help. Soon after, Lisa received a wonderful job offer at a hospice in a neighboring county. It was just the sort of work that she'd dreamed of. Her new boss mentioned that she knew of a home for rent near the hospice.

When she first saw the cottage, Lisa knew that she was home. A small river ran through the front yard, and Lisa drove across a wooden bridge to park in front of the house. Most of the rooms were decorated in the same shade of pink as her portrait of Lilitte, the fairy.

That Christmas, Lisa's wish came true. She was together with her family in her mountain-side cottage, which was decorated with lights, garland, and bows.

Lisa says, "I felt so blessed at Christmas-time. I walked outside to place bright red bows on either side of the wooden bridge and listened to the gentle roar of the river running beneath me. I looked around at the tall trees and thanked God for the privilege of living in the mountains. I began to walk toward the house, where I could see lights and decorations from the tree through my open windows.

"The setting sun hit the bright green tin roof that sheltered my red house. I heard whispering and knew that my fairy was enjoying my joy. My little home looked just like Santa's cottage. I walked back to the house with the sound of fairy wings buzzing in my ears."

Fairies Help with Careers

Not only can fairies help to manifest objects, they can also help with careers, schooling, relationships, and other needs. For example, I was recently stopped at an airport for a security screening. The security personnel put me in a little waiting area and then left. My flight was about to board, and I called upon the angels and ascended masters for help. Still, I waited.

Then finally I closed my eyes and implored, "Fairies and fairy queens! Please help me get out of this waiting area, have a very quick and noninvasive screening, and get on my plane in plenty of time." As soon as I opened my eyes, a woman from security came to retrieve me. She gave me a very casual pat-down and didn't even open my luggage. I thanked the fairies for their speedy, perfect, and very efficient help.

Emily Beevers of England called upon the fairies to help her find a job in her chosen field of addictions counseling:

> Emily visited a local drug-and-alcohol recovery center to ask about volunteer work. Even though the manager knew Emily's father, he still didn't have any volunteer openings to offer her.
>
> When she returned home, Emily consulted her *Healing with the Fairies Oracle Cards*. She received the message that her wish would come true if she was willing to be patient.
>
> Emily felt guided to contact an old friend she hadn't seen for some time. When she talked about her employment search, the friend

produced a newspaper ad that she'd just found that morning. It was for a paid position at another recovery center.

Emily immediately applied and was hired right away. She says, "I couldn't be happier!" She gives full credit to the fairies for guiding her to her dream career.

Not only do the fairies help us realize our dreams, but they also help us pinpoint what our dreams *are*. Some people don't ask for heavenly help because they don't know what they want, or because they're afraid of praying for the "wrong" thing. Mary Diane Hausman discovered that she could turn to the fairies for guidance and also receive their help in following it:

Mary Diane connected with the fairies during a weekend workshop that my husband and I held in upstate New York, a location highly populated with elementals.

She came home from the workshop rejuvenated and inspired to discover her true life's purpose. Weary from having worked in the competitive corporate world for the past 20 years, Mary wracked her brain to find a suitable career to transition into. Still, nothing seemed right, and she wasn't willing to quit her job without a new career to fall back upon.

One day as she went for a walk away from her office during lunchtime, Mary heard a voice instruct her to go inside a candy store and purchase a lottery ticket. She recalls, "This voice was not my own inner guidance. This was a solid, real voice that I could hear inside my head. I knew without a doubt that this was a fairy speaking."

When Mary went into the candy store, the voice said, "Ask for the leprechaun scratch-off numbers." And sure enough, there was a game of little pots of gold with leprechauns on them! She bought a sheet and walked outside. Before she scratched off the numbers, the voice said, quite clearly, "You need to find out about equine massage." Mary had never heard of equine massage and wasn't sure that such an occupation even existed.

Although she didn't win any money from the lottery tickets, Mary realized that the leprechauns and fairies had answered her prayers in a more valuable way. They'd grabbed her attention enough for Mary to hear their guidance about equine massage.

Mary says, "I do love horses and have always fantasized about being around them, yet it just never occurred to me that I could find a way to be with them as a career." As she researched equine massage on the Internet, a whole new world opened up for Mary. In the fall of 2005, Mary became a Certified Equine Sports Massage Therapist.

She says, "My path is much deeper than simply massaging horses. I'm being led to my own healing, as well as healing horses and others, through this path. The entire direction of my life has changed because of the message from the fairies. I do believe with all my heart that it was the fairies speaking to me that day in June. I haven't been so certain or sure of a Divine message and path in a very long time as I have of this one. It has brought me so much comfort and joy. And the fact that I followed it unquestioningly gives me great hope to continue following the voices of the fairies whenever I hear them. Their guidance is unerring and true. I never doubt them."

Fairies Help Find Lost Objects

As with any relationship, you need to initiate the process of receiving help by either requesting it or doing a favor. The fairies are shy beings who are reluctant to reveal their identity or location unless they're assured that you're a sincere person or that they'll receive something in return. Heather R. learned that fairies will help retrieve lost objects if we'll offer a sparkly reward:

Heather looked everywhere for a missing necklace, but it seemed to be lost. So she decided to try a method that a friend had recently shared with her:

She recalls: "You put something shiny like tinfoil under a glass. You then ask the fairies to bring back the lost item in exchange for the shiny thing. In this case, I was looking for a dragonfly necklace. The glass with the balled-up tinfoil sat on my kitchen counter for about a week.

"One day I was picking a pair of shoes out of my closet, and while I was picking them up, the dragonfly necklace flew out of my shoe straight at me. Any lingering doubts I had about fairies completely vanished. I put the tinfoil out in the garden to reward the fairies as promised, and I haven't seen it since!"

Fairies Help Sell Homes

When we decided to sell our home, my husband and I talked with the fairies in our yard. We reassured them, "We promise to only sell this house to a family that will respect you." We asked for wonderful people to buy our home, and love it as much as or more than we had. So when a real-estate agent brought a man named Merlin and his wife and four children to look at the house, we winked at the fairies. We'd found our family, thanks to the fairies!

Like me, Diane Bernier turned to the fairies for help when she decided to sell her house:

> Diane felt a deep connection to the elementals in her backyard, including the butterflies and a particular tree spirit. When it was time for her and her husband to move and sell their home, she asked the tree spirits, fairies, and angels to send a buyer who would love the land and take good care of it. The house was sold five days later to a young farmer.

Asking the Fairies for Help

There are many ways to enlist the fairies' help:

• Go out into nature and speak to the fairies either aloud, silently, with song, or by written letter.

- Give the fairies an offering, such as
  a shiny object or a sweet treat. If you
  leave candy for them, be sure to remove
  the wrapping first. The fairies adore
  chocolate.

- Do something nice for the environment
  or animals, such as recycling; switching
  to Earth-friendly cleaning supplies; re-
  ducing or eliminating animal products
  from your diet; or picking up rubbish.

- Let other people know that fairies are
  real. The fairies are grateful to people
  who teach others about them, because
  the more people who believe in fairies,
  the more power they have to help us all.

Fairies always listen and respond to those who initiate contact. If you've already developed a relationship of mutual trust with the fairies, they'll answer your prayers immediately. If you're new to the fairies, they'll first decide how well you've treated the environment and animals, and if you're a trust-worthy person with pure intentions.

If you pass their test, the fairies will then help you. If not, the fairies will give you an assignment that you'll receive through intuitive feelings, thoughts, or words. Usually, their assignment involves picking up garbage from the great outdoors. Once you pass the fairies' screening process, they'll let you get to know them. Some people even see the fairies, as you'll read about in the next chapter.

Chapter Three

HEALING WITH THE FAIRIES

The fairies are remarkable healers of humans, animals, and plants. Because they're so close to the earth, they have an innate understanding of how to make Earth life better. They understand the physical world, yet are enough above it that they can effect magic and miracles by their very presence.

Peggy Boucharde was healed of a serious illness with the help of a fairy. The one whom Peggy saw immediately before her healing was the size of a young child. Fairies come in a variety of sizes, from very tiny to child-sized. Peggy's fairy also had gossamer, insectlike wings, which is a characteristic distinguishing fairies from angels. Angels have feathery, birdlike wings, while fairies have dragonfly or butterfly wings.

Peggy was in a lot of pain due to an autoimmune disease. She was bedridden, with painful rashes and stomach distress. Her doctors said that there was nothing they could do.

One afternoon as Peggy lay in distress, she noticed movement in the courtyard outside her bedroom window. She raised her head to see a golden-haired child about three or four years old sitting on the outside stairs leading into her bedroom. The girl's hair was full of curls, and her dress had colors like Peggy had never seen before.

Then Peggy noticed that the little girl had wings. They were delicate, insectlike wings, full of color.

As Peggy and the girl looked at each other, Peggy was filled with a peaceful feeling and she fell asleep. When she woke up, her stomach pain was gone. She also remembered an ointment remedy that her mother had used

for rashes many years before. Although her husband didn't believe that she'd seen a fairy, he was grateful that Peggy felt better, so he went to the store to buy the ointment. Soon after, Peggy's rashes healed and disappeared.

She says, "I know I saw a fairy that day, and I'm much better as a result of her healing visit."

The fairies are the master magicians of the physical world, so there's no condition that they can't heal. Anna Waters-Massey of Australia even discovered that the fairies could help her stop hiccupping:

Anna had always struggled with hiccups. She says, "When I have a bout of hiccups that won't go away, I get so fed up."

One day Anna's hiccups became overwhelming. Nothing seemed to work, and that night she couldn't go to sleep because of them. Suddenly the thought came to her: *Ask the fairies for help with your hiccups!* So Anna thought, *Okay, I will.*

As soon as Anna asked the fairies to cure her hiccups, she felt a playful giggling inside and around her. The hiccups immediately ceased, which made Anna giggle with delight.

Anna has since taught her 11-year-old daughter to call upon the fairies for help with hiccups. As with Anna, her daughter has had immediate and lasting success in alleviating the condition, thanks to the fairies.

Ask the fairies for a healing in the same way that you ask them to help you manifest a dream. It's best to talk to them when you're outdoors, although there are fairies wherever there are plants or animals. So you could even stand next to a house plant or your pet while talking to the fairies. You can ask silently, aloud, through song, or a letter.

Healing Other People with the Fairies

You can also request that the fairies help other people. The fairies won't interfere with someone's free will; however, they will help someone who's *open*

to receiving help. Fairies are definitely good-hearted and generous, as Margot Herold discovered:

Margot has introduced the fairies' healing abilities to several people. For instance, she gave a copy of my book *Healing with the Fairies* to a friend who wanted to stop smoking. The friend had tried everything, only to start up again after terrible withdrawal pains and people complaining that she was intolerable.

After reading the book, Margot asked the fairies for help. This time, her friend didn't have any withdrawal symptoms, and no one complained that she was moody. Whenever she felt the urge for a cigarette, she'd ask the fairies for help. Always, she was able to resist. She's now stopped smoking for good, thanks to the fairies.

Next, Margot helped her one-year-old niece, Lara, to heal and sleep through the night with the aid of the fairies. One night, Margot's sister called to say that Lara had been up all night ill, crying, and whining. As soon as the telephone conversation ended, Margot put the girl's

photograph and a rose quartz crystal on the windowsill. She asked the fairies for help and sent love to her niece.

The next morning, Margot's sister called to say that Lara got better immediately after their phone call. She slept through the night and was completely well in the morning.

The Fairies Protect Us from Harsh Elements

Clearly, the fairies are natural physicians who have their finger on the pulse of earthly life. In addition to healing our bodies, the fairies can also protect us from physical harm, especially from harsh elements. Sue Charbonneau and her dog, Rosie, were rescued after she asked the fairies for help:

Sue and Rosie were following the snow-mobile trails in the marshes one February morning near her Ontario, Canada, home. Usually, this hike takes 20 minutes, but that day the snow was soft, and Sue began to sink into the marshes. She hadn't worn boots or

long johns because the hike is normally brief and on hard snow.

As Sue and Rosie's legs sank deeply into the snowy marsh, Sue asked the fairies to help Rosie pull her out. The dog then began tugging on Sue's mitten, which helped her leverage her way out of the hole. Since Rosie's a small 12-pound dog, Sue knew that the fairies had assisted them both.

Sue remembers what happened next: "I had to get back to the firmer trail. I asked the fairies to help me be lightweight so that my feet wouldn't sink any farther. I asked them to help me make it back safely before I got too cold. I tentatively started to walk, and to my amazement, it was as though I was hardly touching the ground. I literally glided the rest of the way until I got to firmer ground. I was so surprised and thankful."

If you ever feel vulnerable to harsh environmental conditions such as snow, wind, water, fire, and

such, call upon the fairies. As the custodians of nature, they can turn physical laws in your favor.

You can ask the fairies to help you in conjunction with any angel or ascended master (such as Archangel Michael, Jesus, Mary, or Buddha) whom you normally call upon. The fairies are nondenominational and happy to work in conjunction with any religious or spiritual principles, especially those that honor nature and animals.

To ask the fairies for healing or protection, simply voice your request aloud, silently, or through written or sung words. They respond instantly to urgent requests (although they may ask you to pick up the garbage on a nature trail later).

Chapter Four

THE FAIRIES
AND ANIMALS

*I*n addition to healing people, the fairies can heal wild and domesticated animals. Fairies are animals' guardian angels. When you pet a dog, cat, or other animal, you're connecting with the fairies. This is one reason why we feel uplifted around animals.

As nature's angels, the fairies are especially fond of helping, healing, and protecting nature's creatures. In fact, you might say that animals are a particular specialty of the fairies. Animals, too, are fond of fairies. Follow your pet's gaze sometime. They're not staring off into vacant space; they're looking at the fairies!

Sue Workman asked the fairies, in particular, a fairy queen named Epona, to help heal her lame horse. A fairy queen is analogous to an archangel or queen bee, in that she organizes the other fairies. Most fairy queens are goddesslike, and they often have areas of interest. For instance, Epona is the fairy queen who helps horses. In Chapter 9, you'll read about the other fairy queens (and kings) and their specialties.

As a small child, Sue spent many hours in the Montana woods connecting with the fairies. She'd leave gifts for them at the base of trees and in the brush. Throughout her adult life, Sue regularly connected with the fairies during her daily nature walks.

Two years ago, the fairies helped Sue and her horse, Moonbeam, in an amazing way. When Sue first adopted Moonbeam, she asked the fairies to protect him. She also called upon Epona, the fairy-queen goddess who watches over horses.

So when Sue found Moonbeam lying in a field with a severely cut foot, she immediately asked Epona and the fairies for help. Moonbeam had cut his foot on barbed wire, and he was struggling to live. Yet moments after she called upon Epona and the fairies, Moonbeam was able to stand on three legs and hobble to the horse trailer.

When they arrived at the veterinarian's office, the news was grim. The doctor, considered one of the best in Montana, gave little hope for Moonbeam's survival and prepared Sue for the worst.

So Sue implored the fairies and Epona to help Moonbeam's spirit through the operation. She asked that Moonbeam not only survive, but fully recover. The next morning, the veterinarian called Sue to say that Moonbeam was standing on his cut foot.

Sue heard the fairies tell her to put the herb golden seal into the mixture that the veterinarian was using to wash Moonbeam's foot with. When Sue asked the doctor if he'd permit this, he said, "Why not? Nothing about this horse makes sense anyway."

The fairies explicitly told Sue how to care for Moonbeam's foot during his recovery. The horse spent two months in a cast and foot wraps. His health and movement is now perfect. Sue gives complete credit for this remarkable recovery to the fairies and Epona.

Like diminutive Doctor Doolittles who make house calls, the fairies can assist with every aspect of pet ownership. They can relieve behavioral challenges, and act as mediators so you'll better understand your pet's needs and concerns. In short, the fairies will help you and your pet develop close and affectionate bonds based on love and mutual understanding.

Help with Squirrels and Mice

In addition to helping with domesticated animals, the fairies are happy to assist you with wild ones. Call upon the fairies if you ever find an injured bird, for instance. The fairies can also protect you from strange dogs and other critters.

If wild animals get into your home, office, or car, the fairies are happy to help. Laurie Montanaro and her husband weren't usually bothered by the squirrels living in their attic, but one day, Laurie needed the fairies' help with one particular squirrel:

Laurie and her husband live in a 50-year-old home in Memphis, complete with squirrels in their attic. One morning a squirrel lost its footing and fell between the walls. She could hear the squirrel struggling to work its way back up to the attic, only to fall back down again. As Laurie listened to the squirrel's panicked scrambling, she wondered how to help.

Laurie remembered reading somewhere that the fairies helped wild animals, so she decided to call upon them. She put her hand on the wall next to the squirrel and asked the fairies to please help guide the little creature back up the wall to safety.

Within minutes, the squirrel successfully made its way up to freedom! Laurie thanked the fairies for their help, and now she always calls upon them to relay messages to domestic and wild animals. She even taught her once-skeptical husband to call upon the fairies for help in a similar situation, and he also experienced success.

Laurie and her husband have learned to live peacefully with the squirrels, thanks to the fairies. Sandy Strommer, however, wasn't happy to share her home with the mice who invaded each winter. Fortunately, the fairies were able to intervene:

Each winter, Sandy's home was invaded by mice trying to find food and escape the outdoor chill. One morning in early December, she opened her cutlery drawer and saw mouse droppings. She didn't have time to start scrubbing her kitchen drawers, so she asked her husband to get rid of the pesky mice. After her husband laid out four mouse traps, though, Sandy had second thoughts. She didn't want to kill the mice. She just wanted them out of her house.

Sandy had recently begun having visions of fairies in her meditations even though she never believed in them. So she read books about fairies, which boosted her confidence in their reality.

Sandy decided to appeal to the fairies for help with the mice. She said, "Fairies, we can't have mice in the house. We don't dislike them if they're outside, but their droppings can spread disease to us humans, and that's why we can't have them in our home. I don't have the time to keep cleaning and disinfecting my kitchen cabinets, so can you please ask them to leave? I don't want to send them out in the cold, but we don't have a choice except to kill them if they're in our house. Please help with this situation because I don't know what else to do. Thank you."

Since that day, Sandy has never had mice in her house again. So when her sister-in-law complained of mice in her home, Sandy called on the fairies to help again, with the same immediate success. She hasn't yet told her sister-in-law why the mice suddenly vacated her house.

Sandy says, "I just love my fairies. They're so much fun!"

So the fairies are wonderfully helpful for anything involving animals. They'll even help you find lost pets or locate a new one for adoption. The fairies will also assist you in sharing the planet peacefully with other living creatures such as plants and trees, as you'll read about in the next chapter.

Chapter Five

GARDENING
AND THE FAIRIES

*W*herever you find flowers, trees, grass, animals, or water, fairies are nearby. Nature is the fairies' domain, home, and temple. They're especially fond of lush vegetation, grown without pesticides or much pruning. So it makes sense that the fairies would help our lawns flourish. All we have to do is invite the fairies to help our gardens grow.

Creating a Fairy Garden

You can attract more fairies into your yard by creating a "fairy garden." This basically means adding what the fairies like to your yard. The fairies will help your garden become a lush, gorgeous sanctuary and a peaceful oasis. Here are some of the elements of a fairy garden:

Flowers. Fairies adore flowers. They also tend to them, ensuring that you'll always have a colorful yard. The fairies love bell-shaped flowers such as bluebells, fritillary, foxglove, and lily of the valley, as they provide wonderful shelter for them. Legends also say that fairies use primrose and cowslip flowers to cross between the physical and nonphysical dimensions.

Chemical-free flora. Fairies are allergic to chemicals, so avoid any pesticides or other sprays that would cause your fairies to scramble to find a new place to live. Most health-food stores sell natural alternatives to pesticides, made from gentle ingredients such as orange peel and herbs. Ask the fairies to help with pest control instead of using chemicals.

A natural environment. Fairies also prefer gardens that are as natural as possible, so keep pruning to a minimum. Tightly manicured gardens and lawns have fewer fairies in residence compared to lush gardens and lawns. Be sure to warn the fairies before walking on grass, and give them an ample heads-up before mowing the lawn.

Feathered and furry friends. The fairies love to share their garden with birds, butterflies, and squirrels. The fairies will amply reward you for keeping a bird feeder in your yard, especially one for hummingbirds (avoid artificial coloring or other harmful chemicals in the liquid). If burrowing animals (such as groundhogs) become a nuisance, ask the fairies to help. You can attract butterflies by planting asters, buddleia, marigolds, lilacs, lavender, and rosemary.

Crystals. Fairies love sparkling crystals, so hang some from monofilament (fishing) line in your trees, and place crystals throughout the yard. Crystals come from the same elemental kingdom as the fairies. Along the same lines, small white lights strung through your trees are a favorite among the fairies.

Fairy furniture and circles. You might place tiny fairy furniture made from wrapped willow wood or borrowed from old dollhouses in the yard. A circle of freshly picked flowers or smooth stones creates a "fairy circle," which is a gathering spot where fairies enter other dimensions together.

Music. You can also place outdoor stereo speakers in the yard (some are built to look like small boulders and rocks). Play gentle music for the plants, flowers, birds, butterflies, and fairy inhabitants to enjoy. Just don't play any harsh music in your yard or you may experience a mass exodus of your garden's residents. Don't be surprised to hear music playing in your yard, especially late at night. The fairies hold parties almost every evening, during which they fiddle, sing, and create fun and danceable music.

Statues. Fairies also appreciate your placing statues of them in your yard. Not only are these statues attractive to fairies, they're also beneficial to nearby plants, as Margot Herold of Germany discovered:

Margot noticed a spot in her flower bed where nothing seemed to grow well. This was in contrast to her front yard, where beautiful roses flourished near a fairy statue that she'd bought on an intuitive hunch even though she didn't believe in fairies at the time.

So Margot bought a fairy statue for the dead spot in her backyard. She also asked the fairies to help her plants grow. Almost immediately, the plants began to thrive. Soon the statue became so overgrown with plants that Margot could no longer see it. Today, she very openly gives credit to the fairies for her beautiful garden.

As you invite the fairies into your garden, you'll notice that everything grows more lush and beautiful. Judy Phillips of Wisconsin has flowers growing in her yard well past the normal blooming season, thanks to the fairies. She's also learned that they're wonderful for pest control:

Judy was distraught when insects kept attacking and eating the plants and flowers in her garden, so she sat in her yard and asked the insects to allow her trees and flowers to bloom and grow. When that didn't work, Judy felt even more frustrated.

In desperation, she decided to ask the fairies for help. She added a little gnome statue to her garden and asked the fairies to keep the bugs away so that the flowers and perennials would get a good start.

Judy says, "Well, my goodness, did the fairies ever come and help me! All the little holes from the pests' chewing disappeared. The flowers grew in thick, healthy, and lovely."

Judy also credits the fairies for helping her garden thrive during the cold Wisconsin winters. Her flowers bloom well into December, even after it's snowed.

Plant Physicians

We've already seen how fairies can heal humans and animals with illnesses and injuries. Since nature

is the fairies' home turf, it's not surprising that they can also heal ailing plants and trees. The fairies healed Linda Dunwoody's tree after it was struck by lightning and pronounced dead by tree specialists:

Linda and her family were awakened one night by a fierce thunder-and-lightning storm, and a loud explosion set off the house alarm system. When the family went outside to investigate, they discovered that a lightning bolt had struck a hundred-year-old pecan tree in their yard. The lightning had continued underground until it blew out the control box for their sprinkler system.

The lightning had blown one side of the tree's bark into splinters, which had hit the house and windows 50 feet away. The entire side of the tree was white, stripped of its protective bark.

Linda contacted several tree experts, who all stated that the tree was dead. The experts said it would cost thousands of dollars to remove the tree, but Linda didn't care about the money. She just didn't want to lose the tree that she'd loved and admired for so many years. Her neighbors had always remarked, "Oh you live in that house with the beautiful pecan tree."

Finally, one expert advised against cutting down the tree. He told Linda to wait until springtime to see if leaves grew as a sign of life. He said that it would be a miracle if the tree lived, but that it was worth trying.

Filled with hope, Linda decided to ask the fairies to heal her pecan tree. She recalls, "Every day I'd ask the fairies to save the tree. My friends and neighbors laughed at me as I'd tell them that the fairies would help the tree to live. I didn't care, though. The important thing was my tree."

The next spring, the pecan tree produced leaves all over. It also began producing more pecans than it had during the 16 years Linda and her family had lived in the home. Now Linda's husband believes in fairies, too! The tree lives on and is home to many squirrels.

Linda's story illustrates that the more we believe in fairies, the more power they have to help trees, animals, plants, and other aspects of nature (including people). Throughout the incident, Linda never doubted that the fairies could heal her tree. And they did!

Like Linda, Su Foh Yau turned to the fairies to heal her ailing pear tree:

> The pear tree in Su's backyard wasn't doing very well. For many years, it would bear lots of flowers, but the pears would turn black and drop to the ground when they were still very tiny. The leaves also turned black.
>
> Su didn't know what to do until she read about the fairies. She went outside and said to them, "My pear tree is sick, and I don't want to spray it with toxic chemicals. Please heal my pear tree and give me lots of pears."
>
> The tree healed right away and bore lots of pears that summer. Su thanks the fairies for tending to her pear tree and granting her wishes.

Evidence of Fairies

Once you invite fairies into your garden, you'll begin seeing evidence of their residence:

- More flowers will bloom.

- Your flowers will be bigger, more colorful, and last longer.

- Birds and squirrels will frequently visit your yard.

- Beautiful butterflies will flutter around your flowers.

- Dragonflies, frogs, and lizards, who are cousins to fairies, may pop in for occasional visits (if you'd prefer not to have reptiles or squirrels visit your yard, simply tell the fairies so).

- Your garden will exude a feeling of peacefulness and be an inviting sanctuary.

"Fairy rings" are another sign of the fairies' presence. When circles of toadstools, mushrooms, or flowers appear in your yard, it's a positive sign that the fairies have taken up permanent residence. Fairies and other elementals (such as leprechauns) travel between dimensions through these rings. If you listen carefully, you can hear music and laughter at night emanating from the circle.

A young Australian woman named Tara wanted to connect with the fairies, so she stood in her garden and invited them to live in her yard. The next morning, Tara found a newly sprouted circle of toadstools in the place she'd stood when she issued the invitation.

Tara's excitement soon turned to sadness when her father mowed the fairy ring down. Very upset, Tara told her father that he'd ruined the fairies' home. Fortunately, the fairies didn't let the situation keep them down. The next day, their ring of toadstools reappeared in the same location as if it had always been there.

Now five years later, Tara's father doesn't mow that part of the yard. There's a baby oak tree, long grass, and several rings in the section of the garden where the fairies live.

Tara says, "That's such a peaceful spot to sit and ponder since my new fairy friends have made themselves at home. My garden is now so vibrant! I visit the fairies daily and tell them everything. I can always feel their loving energy surrounding and healing me."

Young people like Tara seem to connect more easily with fairies than do adults. Many have told me that they saw fairies when they were children. As they grew up and began to doubt the fairies' existence and stay indoors more often, their connection dimmed.

Fortunately, today's children are more often raised by open-minded parents who believe and encourage interactions with fairies and angels. You'll see in the next chapter that the fairies hold a special place in the hearts of children.

Chapter Six

CHILDREN
AND THE FAIRIES

*I*t seems that we're all becoming more sensitive, and children are no exception. I'm constantly amazed and awed by the profound depth of spiritual understanding that kids naturally display. At nearly all of my workshops, I meet boys and girls who tell me about their encounters with fairies and angels. These children not only believe in fairies, they *know* that they're real.

In past decades, some parents were frightened when their children would discuss invisible friends. Today, parents accept and even encourage their offspring's spiritual gifts. Many parents bring their children to my psychic-development courses even though most of these young people are so spiritually gifted that they don't need much instruction. They already see the spirit world, and they trust their visions and intuitive feelings.

One reason why children see fairies so easily is because the fairies trust them. They know that children have pure hearts and loving intentions, so they reveal themselves to these young people.

The fairies even left physical evidence of their presence for young Sydnee Teets:

> Amy Teets raised her children to speak honestly about their spiritual visions and visitations, and not to be swayed by skeptics. As a result, her daughter Sydnee has strong clairvoyant abilities that she openly discusses.
>
> When Sydnee was in preschool, she constantly talked about her friend Becky, who was very small, had brown skin, and purple wings. Becky lived in a white rock and could climb up the walls with her sticky hands.
>
> One day after school, Amy noticed a perfect little purple handprint on Sydnee's sock. At first, Amy scolded Sydnee for getting paint

on her clothes. Sydnee was quick to correct her mother's assumption and said, "I didn't do it. Becky did it. You know, Mom, my fairy!"

Sydnee says that the fairies and angels teach her about colors. They've taught Sydnee to stay away from people with certain colors in their aura such as orange, gray, or black.

Sydnee's sock, complete with a tiny purple handprint.

Amy Teet's hand next
to the sock shows how tiny the handprint is.

Fairies Help Children Feel Safe and Happy

Fairies will do anything they can to help children. The fairies' love for kids motivates them to guide, protect, and help in any way they can. Many parents report success in calling upon both angels and fairies to assist with their children, as Karen Gore of Ireland discovered:

Karen's four-year-old son, Kodi, wasn't coping well at school. He cried every day and would draw paintings of scary monsters and dark colors. In desperation, Karen decided to call upon angels and fairies to help her son. As she dropped Kodi off at school, Karen explained that today would be better because the angels would look after him. She didn't mention that she'd also asked the fairies to watch over him. As Karen left the school, a tiny white feather floated by her head, which gave her a feeling of peace.

When Karen picked Kodi up after school, she asked him how his day had gone. "Fine, Mummy," he replied. "No tears today!"

Karen asked him who'd looked after him in the playground, leaving it open for Kodi to answer whether it was his sister, a teacher, or the angels. Karen was completely surprised when Kodi said that the fairies had kept him company.

Kodi explained that he'd seen loads of them: boy fairies, girl fairies, and even little baby ones. They stayed with him in his classroom, too.

Kodi had seen fairies on the roof, on the windowsills, and on his desk. One fairy even tickled him on his back.

Karen was pleasantly shocked, since she hadn't spoken to Kodi about fairies. Since that day, Kodi's artwork has changed. Bright colors have replaced the dark hues and scary monsters that he once obsessively drew. Instead, he soon drew a beautiful picture of his house, surrounded by a rainbow and little yellow orbs, which Karen knew were the fairies. Kodi also drew a portrait of his fairy, complete with huge green eyes and little whiskers.

Karen says, "Kodi sees his fairies everywhere now, and he often tells me where they are in our home. He's much more settled now, and has even started socializing without me. Thank you, fairies, for your help!"

The fairies helped Kodi feel safe and understood. This freed Kodi to let go of his fear-based behaviors. As a result, he enjoys himself more and is much more pleasant to be with.

You can ask the fairies to help you with any child-hood emotional or behavioral issue, including phobias, as Susan Rust did:

The fairies helped Susan's three-and-a-half-year-old son, Blake, overcome a phobia of being in the water. He wouldn't even put his feet into the lake during family outings. Then one day he began laughing in the bathtub. He told his mother, "I'm pretending that I'm drowning."

When his horrified mother asked him why, Blake replied, "Because my fairies told me to."

Susan thought that his fairies had a strange sense of humor until she later realized that they were helping her son overcome his fear of drowning. The next time they visited the lake, Blake wasn't afraid of the water at all.

At night when Susan puts her son to bed and things are quieting down in the house, she notices Blake staring or communicating with his fairies and angels.

One night Susan walked into her son's room to read him a bedtime story. Blake greeted her with a lot of happiness and excitement. Smiling, he said, "Mommy, I can do magic with my hands! My fairies showed me!"

At first Susan wondered what kind of magic tricks a three-year-old could do, but she asked Blake to show her what he meant. He then placed his hand on Susan's forehead for a short time. After he pulled his hands off, he said, "Okay, that's enough." Susan then realized that the fairies had taught him how to do hands-on healing.

The fairies enjoy teaching children about the magic of earthly life. They mentor children about ways to manifest instantly and how to heal, as they did with Blake. The fairies make wonderfully patient teachers, as well as counselors and coaches.

You can tell the fairies about your worries and fears, or ask them to help you with any need. When you pour your heart out to the fairies, they not only listen, but they also intervene by bringing about a solution. They'll even help children's dreams, such as career aspirations, come true:

Although Gabrielle Lisa Baglia is a student of the psychic arts, she'd never given any thoughts to fairies. So she was shocked when a foot-high brunette female fairy appeared before her eyes one day. The fairy wore a pink dress and had beautifully colored transparent wings, which beat faster than a hummingbird's. The fairy began dancing gracefully and then stopped and said in a sweet, wee voice: "Integrity." Then she disappeared.

Gabrielle concluded that she was seeing things because she was overly tired. Still, a part of her believed that she'd really seen a fairy. She wondered what the fairy meant by uttering the word *integrity*.

Soon after she arrived at work, Gabrielle's husband called her and said, "Guess what? Integrity Casting called for Elizabeth!" Their five-year-old daughter dreamed of becoming an Oscar-winning actress, and that day, the agency offered Elizabeth a contract.

Gabrielle noticed that the fairy appeared, or she heard fairy giggling, every time the casting agent was about to call. Gabrielle says,

"She also appears when I need to manifest money in an instant. In the summer of 2005, I needed a down payment for a car, and she appeared in a bigger-than-normal size, like an eight-year-old child. The same day that she made her grand entrance, I received a direct deposit out of the blue in my bank account for $4,000. This money was owed to me from a few years back. I was so happy and grateful for the miracle this little being assisted in providing! This kind of thing happens all the time when I see my little fairy guide."

Elizabeth has been in commercials, and she models a West Coast designer's fashion line. Gabrielle gives full credit to the fairy.

Of course, the fairies help adults as well as children. Men and women with open minds and hearts who are kind to nature's creatures can garner the fairies' assistance simply by asking for it.

Sometimes the fairies help when we're least expecting it, as you'll read about next.

Chapter Seven

THE FAIRIES
AND SCHOOL

*W*hen I began collecting true stories about fairies, I was pleased but not surprised by how many people received the fairies' help with their gardens and pets. After all, nature is the fairies' domain. What did surprise me was discovering how many times fairies helped students with their schoolwork. I'd never realized before how much fairies valued education!

Yet it does make sense that the fairies would help us finance our education, since they're brilliant at manifesting whatever material needs are required. Anna Dean was thrilled when the fairies helped her win a scholarship so that she could attend graduate school:

As a child, Anna played and talked with fairies in her garden. She lost this connection by listening to people who told her to "grow up and stop talking to imaginary friends." But as an adult, she rediscovered the fairies. Anna knew that they were with her to help fulfill her life's purpose of environmentalism.

Anna's fairy friends helped her secure a paid research position, guaranteeing that she'd have enough money to pay for her first year of graduate education. However, Anna was unsure how she'd finance her second year of school.

A clairvoyant healer told Anna one day, "I see fairies all around you, holding up fists stuffed with money. They want you to ask them for it, and to be specific!"

The following week, Anna saw an announce-ment about a fellowship offered through her graduate program. She knew that she was quali-fied to win it, but she also realized that there would be many competitive applicants. Anna says, "Right then and there I asked the fairies for that fellowship."

She could feel and hear the fairies assisting her in writing the fellowship application. They asked her to wait, and trust that they would follow through and help her win. Whenever Anna worried about the fellowship, the fairies would reassure her. So she continued to put her full faith in them.

Anna's trust in her fairy friends was rewarded when she learned that she'd won the fellowship! She says, "I thanked the fairies endlessly, and vowed to always trust my elemental friends. As a token of my everlasting gratitude toward them, I now wear a silver fairy charm around my neck and close to my heart. If I may say one other thing to readers, it's to believe and trust in these magnificent creatures, and they will bless your life."

Scholarly Fairies

In the previous chapter, you read about Kodi, the little boy who was helped by the fairies to cope at school. Even though Kodi's mother had invoked both the angels and the fairies to help him, the boy saw only fairies. After his encounter, Kodi became happy and well adjusted. The story points to one reason why

FAIRIES 101

fairies may be so effective for children: because they can relate to one another.

Fairies and children share many qualities, such as wide-eyed enthusiasm for life, playfulness, and an openness to magic. Yet the fairies can help adults who have these characteristics as well.

As children, we didn't worry if a vision stemmed from our imagination. If we saw it, it was real. As we grew older, we may have become wary of anything "imaginary," so we shut off our ability to see fairies and other clairvoyant visions.

Yet you don't have to see fairies in order to receive their help. You just need to be open-minded, as Rena Schmoeller discovered:

> Rena was studying for a very difficult school exam. That night, she saw a vision of a face made of green leaves. She felt as if the spirit of the plant on her study desk were merging with her own spirit. Then Rena received downloads of consolidated information from the plant spirit, as if he were her study buddy reminding her of all that they'd learned together. Rena passed the exam with high marks. A year later, she found a painting of the leafy face she'd seen the night before her exam. It was "the Green Man."

Rena says, "I'm still feeling very blessed by the support I received from him."

The Green Man, who oversees the tree spirits.

The Green Man is a very powerful and loving elemental who oversees the tree spirits, which is a topic we'll delve into in the next chapter.

Chapter Eight

THE SPIRIT OF NATURE

As we've seen, fairies are powerful healers, magicians, and teachers. Anyone who works with fairies begins to realize that everything on this planet is alive, including seemingly inanimate objects like rocks. The omnipresent spirit of love and light is embodied throughout nature. God is everywhere. This spirit is manifested in many forms, including people, animals, plants, and the elemental kingdom.

Tree Spirits

We briefly discussed tree spirits in the last chapter. The term may sound odd, yet haven't you seen faces in the knots and patterns of tree bark? Old oak- and pine-tree trunks look like elderly gentlemen when viewed with an open mind. These faces are the spirits of the trees.

I loved how director Peter Jackson portrayed tree spirits in his *Lord of the Rings* film trilogy. The Ents, as *Rings* author Tolkien termed the tree spirits, looked and talked just like the tree spirits that I (and other open-minded people) see.

Trees have long been associated with spirituality, divination, and healing. The ancient Celtic Druids are known as "the people of the tree knowledge." They derived their wisdom from oak trees, their rune stone system is said to be based upon symbols they received from trees, and they held their ceremonies in groves. Socrates also regarded oak trees as oracles who could tell the future and reveal important information.

Other trees considered sacred and as symbols of deities include the willow, pine, olive, and laurel. In fact, white willow bark was the original basis for aspirin. Jesus' uncle Joseph of Arimathea walked with a staff made from a holy thorn-tree branch. When his staff was placed at the gardens of Chalice Well in Glastonbury, England, it grew into a living tree. Each year, the tree blooms at Christmastime, and its flowers are said to have healing properties. Pine trees are associated with the holy days of Yule and Christmas, and pine oil is a natural pain-relieving ointment.

Tree spirits are the soul and spirit that inhabit each tree, just as your soul and spirit inhabits your body. Each tree spirit has a different personality, complete with quirks and personal tastes. Developing a connection with a tree spirit is as rewarding as any other relationship. You'll build mutual trust and help and protect each other. Perhaps most important, tree spirits help us develop a deeper bond with, and respect for, nature in general.

Laura Bolotin of Grand Junction, Colorado, has always loved trees and believed in tree spirits. In the fall of 2003, Laura met one very special tree spirit in Glade Park, Colorado:

As she and her husband were hiking, Laura felt a very strong presence. At the top of the ridge, they found a huge 40-foot ponderosa pine tree. Laura felt an immediate connection with the tree.

She says, "It wasn't just the size of this tree that drew me. It was the incredible grand-fatherly energy that came from it. I told my husband that I wanted to sit with the tree for a while."

Laura then engaged in a process that she calls "blending with the tree spirit." First, she wrapped her arms around the trunk and asked the tree's permission to blend her spirit with it. She says, "I've found that most trees require several visits before they're ready for this kind of sharing. But this spirit was different, and he said yes right away."

So Laura sat down between two of the tree roots, with her back resting against the trunk. As her own spirit blended with the tree's spirit, Laura began receiving visions from the tree's history. She estimated that the mental movies she saw came from 150 years past, judging by the wagons and clothing of the people she saw in the visions.

When the tree was finished sharing its memories with Laura, they simply exchanged energy back and forth. She says, "This is a very relaxing process, and I've found that many trees will try to heal you if you're tired or hurt."

Since that day, Laura has made regular visits to her tree friend. On one visit, she received a steady stream of visions about pine cones. She saw herself picking them up and taking them home. So she picked up one pine cone at the end of their visit. Still, she felt as if the tree were laughing at her and wondered what it meant.

A few days later, a friend asked Laura if she knew where to get a large quantity of pine cones for some holiday gifts she was making. That's when Laura understood the message she'd received from her tree friend. She wasn't supposed to take just *one* pine cone. No wonder the tree had laughed!

The next day when she visited the tree, she could feel his humor. Laura took home 50 pounds of pine cones. She thanked the tree for his generous gifts, and to this day she continues to visit him as much as possible.

In my book *Goddesses & Angels*, I discussed how a banyan tree spirit in Brisbane, Australia, helped me during a grueling international book tour. I felt exhausted and physically depleted one day while walking through the Brisbane Botanical Gardens. I'd just completed a multicity tour that included many late-night workshops and lots of plane travel.

I felt drawn toward one particular banyan tree. There was nothing apparently special about the tree, in that it wasn't larger or prettier than the other trees of its kind, yet I felt called to lean next to it. I then heard some subtle but clear guidance from the tree. It guided me to put my back completely flush against its trunk. I felt the tree extract my fatigue and the onset of a cold from my body. The amount of love that surrounded this process was indescribable. When it was complete, I stood up, feeling renewed and completely well. I thanked the tree for its loving, healing work.

Nature Spirits

Just as each tree has a spirit and a soul, so does each plant. You can see the faces within each bush and flower. One reason why fairies are such successful gardeners is that they acknowledge and honor these plant spirits. You can develop personal relationships with the plants in your garden by communicating with them, either silently or aloud. The plants hear your words, and they appreciate any kindness you extend their way, such as sincere compliments and tender care.

If you ask your plants, "What do you need?" they'll answer you. Trust the response you receive in your heart, feelings, thoughts, or visions. You may hear that the plant needs shielding from harsh sunlight or your dog's enthusiastic digging. Or the plant may ask for more water or fertilizer. As an intuitive gardener, you work in partnership with the fairies.

Crystals and Rocks

Crystals amplify energy. That's why they're used to boost the efficiency of quartz watches, computers, hair dryers, and other appliances. So it's no surprise that crystals, rocks, and other minerals contain energy. You can see faces in rocks, as well as in the lines of sliced marble and granite. These are the souls and spirits that inhabit the mineral kingdom.

≈

It takes a compassionate heart and open mind to connect with the spirits of the land. Those who won't acknowledge the life force within nature are often the ones who abuse the environment and animals. They don't want to know that the spirit within nature is the same spirit that animates every human. So don't expect everyone to understand your connection with nature spirits. Your relationship with the elemental realm may be a deeply personal connection. Enjoy the magic, and share it with other sensitive and compassionate individuals as you feel guided.

☙❧

Chapter Nine

FLOWER FAIRIES AND OTHER ELEMENTALS

*J*ust as there are many types of angels within the "angelic realm," so do many different beings come from the family of the "elemental realm." As we've discussed, the term *elemental* refers to the beings who watch over the elements of water, air, earth, and fire.

Virtually every culture holds beliefs and myths about elemental spirits. While we commonly think of fairies as Celtic in origin, similar beings are described in Greek, Asian, African, Mediterranean, Native American, Pacific, Polynesian, Nordic, and Teutonic cultures. In fact, the Brothers Grimm, who popularized fairy tales, were German.

Here are some of the elementals you might encounter and call upon:

Brownies: These are kind and helpful wingless beings, usually male. You can ask for a "house brownie" to live with you and watch over your home and occupants, as he'll be a trustworthy companion. Be sure to leave food and drink out for him each night in exchange for his house-sitting work.

Devas: These tiny beings often appear as orbs or colored lights in nature photographs. Devas assist all living beings, including animals and humans. You can call upon body devas to help with health and beauty concerns. You can ask the weather devas for help with rainfall, air temperature, and wind.

Dryads: This is another term for tree spirits or tree people. These beings are the life-force spirits within trees.

Elves: These are large, wingless, human-looking elementals who are wonderful craftsmen. They're usually very kind and helpful, although "trooping elves" (those who travel in bands with other elves) are considered nicer than solitary elves. Call upon them to help you with sewing, knitting, or any other artistic project.

Flower fairies: These are beautiful, tiny fairies who help flowers grow. Like other fairies, they have butterfly or dragonfly wings.

Gnomes: These are elderly-looking male and female dwarfs who are sweet-tempered, kind, and helpful. Male gnomes usually have long beards. Gnomes are wonderful gardeners, and if you place a gnome statue in your yard, it will flourish beautifully.

Leprechauns: Child-sized, wingless elementals, they're the original inhabitants of Ireland who shape-shifted into little people during the Gaelic invasion. They were once called the Tuatha de Dananns (the "people of the Goddess Dana"). Leprechauns are very helpful toward humans they respect (they're partial to lighthearted environmentalists and musicians), and can be mischievous (but never malevolent) toward others. Some people have a leprechaun as a personal spirit guide. Because they're large and close to the earth's density, leprechauns are among the easiest of the elementals to see with your physical eyes, especially if you visit the Irish countryside.

Menehune: These are small, wingless, human-looking nature spirits found in the Polynesian and Hawaiian islands.

Mermaids, mermen, and merpeople: Water-dwelling elementals who live in oceans and lakes, their faces and upper torsos are human, while their lower halves consist of a fish body and tail. Female merpeople are called "mermaids," and the males are called "mermen." Merpeople help humans who are kind to the ocean and ocean-dwelling creatures.

Nymphs: This is the Greek name for beautiful female nature fairies who oversee the waters (water nymphs) and woods (wood nymphs). Because of the elementals' love for parties, song, dance, and romance, people with strong sexual appetites are often called "nymphomaniacs" or "nymphs."

Pixies: These are thin, tall, short-haired winged elementals who love to help plants and flowers grow with their magical "pixie dust." They're sweet, friendly, and playful. You'll know that pixies have been in your garden when you see trails of metallic dust. Pixie haircuts were named after their bobbed hairstyles.

Sea sprites (see *Undines*)

Selkies: Mermaids who appear as seals while in the ocean and as female humans while on land, they're most commonly found in Scotland. In Ireland, they're called Roanes. Selkies help fishermen and sailors.

Sidhe: This is a Gaelic word referring to elementals, and it's pronounced *SHEE*. The term is derived from the Hindi language, and it originally meant "forces that control the elements." Today, *sidhe* is defined as "little people of the fairy mounds or hills."

Sylphs: These are tiny, light-colored, winged beings who govern and live in the element of air. The physician

Paracelsus described them as the mediators between physical beings and air. Call upon the sylphs to increase or decrease the wind.

Undines: This is the Greek term for "sea sprites." They're tiny, light-colored, wingless beings who govern and live in water. You can see and hear them playing in the sea spray of the ocean.

Fairy Queens and Kings

The beings who oversee the elementals are called fairy queens and fairy kings. Some of them are so powerful that they're classified as goddesses and deities. You can ask these benevolent royals to help you with any situation that they specialize in:

Aine (usually pronounced *AHN-yaw* or *Ah-nay*): She's an Irish fairy queen who's especially strong and honored during summertime. Aine is a powerful and loving fertility goddess whom you can call upon for help with your gardens, relationships, and abundance.

Cordelia: She's a beautiful flower fairy queen who oversees the blossoming of flowers each spring and summer. You can ask Cordelia to help your garden flowers to bloom.

Dakinis: The elementals who assist Hindu goddesses and gods, they also assist people who practice yoga. They're also known as Khadomas in Tibet.

Dana (usually pronounced *DAWN-yah*): The original people of Ireland worshiped Dana as their mother goddess. They were called "the people of Dana," or the Tuatha de Dananns. When the Gaelics threatened to invade Ireland, the Tuathas asked Dana whether they should run or fight. She gave them a third choice, which they accepted: to be turned into little people called leprechauns so that they could peacefully coexist with the Gaelics and remain in Ireland. Call upon Dana for wise solutions and insights, increased power, fertility, and abundance.

Epona: This is the Celtic and Roman fairy queen who protects, heals, and guides horses, mules, and donkeys. Call upon Epona for anything involving horses or equestrianism.

Finvarra: The original Irish king of the leprechauns and the Tuatha de Dananns, he's the husband of Oonagh. Call upon Finvarra to develop a closer connection to leprechauns or to ask for your own personal leprechaun spirit guide.

Flora: The Greek and Roman fairy goddess of springtime, flowers, and fertility, she's wonderful to call upon if you're having a garden party or just want to elevate the mood of any gathering.

Green Man: He oversees and protects forests and woods. He also helps trees reproduce and grow. His image is depicted in paintings and statues as a man's face peering through oak leaves. Call upon the Green Man to help your trees heal and grow.

Holly King: The overseer of holly trees, he rules the forests and woods during the fall and winter seasons. Call upon the Holly King to help you to rest, reflect, and retreat. (Also see *Oak King*.)

Maeve: She's a powerful and loving fairy queen who works with body devas to help women with menstrual, menopausal, and other feminine physical issues.

Nemetona: She's the queen of tree spirits, especially oaks and other sacred trees. Call upon Nemetona to help your garden become a sacred sanctuary for prayer and meditation.

Oak King: The guardian of oak trees, he rules the forests and woods during the spring and summer months. Call upon the Oak King to help you with new projects and anything involving growth, renewal, and birth. (Also see *Holly King.*)

Oonagh (or Onaugh): She and her husband, Finvarra, were the original queen and king of the Tuatha de Dananns (see *Dana*). Since she's renowned for her lustrous, long hair, you can call upon Oonagh for help with your own locks. She's also wonderful to call upon for issues involving monogamy and affairs in relationships, since Oonagh endured her own trials with betrayal in her marriage.

Pan: The Grecian half-goat male deity who oversees and protects woods, pastures, shepherds, and livestock, he's a symbol of mirth, playfulness, and fertility who was demonized during repressive eras in human history.

Chapter Ten

CONNECTING
WITH THE
FAIRIES

*S*ince fairies are everywhere, you can connect with them at any time. However, it's easiest to hear and see the fairies where they congregate outside in nature, or wherever there are lots of plants or animals. The more fairies there are, the easier they are to hear and see.

The fairies are as real as you are, and they'd love to help you. To connect with them, first decide on a question or request to ask. Direct this request to them, either aloud or silently. The fairies hear every request from every being, even those who are new to working with elementals.

Before the fairies can reply to or help you, they'll first need to know more about your relationship to the environment and animals. They can access this information instantaneously from the energy field surrounding your body.

The fairies aren't judging you so much as they're assessing how Earth-friendly your attitudes, beliefs, and behaviors are. If they deem that you need improvements in this area, the fairies will give you assignments. For instance, you may receive gut feelings to recycle your rubbish, or to pick up garbage from a nature path. If you follow these intuitive callings, the fairies will begin helping you and working with you.

As long as you do your best to display kindness toward the environment and animals, the fairies will do whatever they can to help you. And remember that if the fairies ask you to purchase Earth-friendly cleaning supplies, you can ask them to help you pay for them!

Seeing the Fairies

You can feel the fairies' presence around plants and animals. Fairies always elicit feelings of excitement, playfulness, and high energy. They're happy, fiery beings.

You can also see evidence of the fairies' presence in your garden, through increased numbers of flowers, butterflies, birds, dragonflies, and foliage.

Once the fairies learn to trust you, they'll allow you to see them. At first you might see the fairies in your mind's eye as tiny sparkling lights, flitting fireflies, or little winged people. These mental images are valid and trustworthy representations of the fairies, yet it's also exciting to see the fairies with your physical eyes. Many children report seeing fairies. The adults who physically see them tend to be outside in nature.

"Fairy lights" are the energy fields surrounding the fairies. They're little twinkling and sparkling lights appearing in meadows, gardens, and forests. These lights move in unusual ways and are also the easiest way to begin seeing fairies with your physical sight:

Eighteen-year-old Adrienne Gallaway and her fiancé, Travis, were hiking in the Garden of the Gods in Illinois. They both picked up litter along the way, apologizing to the fairies and plants for other people's negligence.

The couple sat on a secluded cliff sheltered by trees and let their feet dangle from the edge. They watched the sun set and the full moon rise. The air was warm and the forest was alive. As they sat, dazzled by the beautiful scenery, Adrienne noticed streaks of light quickly move past her. Most of the lights were white, but a few were colored blue and red. The streaks began to take on more form and a larger size.

Adrienne didn't say anything to Travis at first because she'd never experienced visions before. Then Travis asked Adrienne if she'd seen anything unusual. Adrienne reluctantly described the streaking lights. To her surprise and relief, Travis excitedly said that he'd seen the same thing!

Adrienne says, "We both commented that we felt very protected and blessed, and not at all afraid of the lights. We sat for a while watching the fairies fly all around us. As we later walked the trail, I had an intense feeling of peace and bliss. I was so happy and so excited that I just wanted to run into the forest and

dance. The farther we went, the stronger this longing to frolic in the forest and celebrate life became.

"We stood next to the car for a long amount of time just staring off into the forest, and neither of us wanted to leave. We heard the sound of large wings buzz loudly around us every once in a while. As I looked at the trees, I kept seeing these white shapes dancing around the thin trees up the hill. To this day, I haven't had a more intense and vivid experience than I did that night, and I still feel highly blessed to have seen what I did."

The fact that both Travis and Adrienne saw the fairy lights together adds validity to their visions. Both were reluctant to admit to the other what they'd seen. Once they discovered that the other person was also seeing the fairy lights, their experience deepened.

Beverly Haupt also saw a fairy light one evening:

One cool February evening, Beverly felt very relaxed and peaceful as she gazed out of her bedroom window at the night sky. She noticed a little golden light out of the corner of her eye. She thought, *What a pretty ember from the fireplace drifting in the night air.*

Beverly continued watching the ember swirl, glide, and move in very unusual ways. She thought, *It's almost as if the ember has control over its movements.* That's when she realized that her fireplace wasn't lit that night.

The ember continued dancing through the air. It dipped and spun toward the window where it traveled the length of the seven-foot-long glass in a perfectly straight line. Beverly says, "It was as if the ember was peeking into my window!"

When the ember was directly in front of Beverly, it stopped moving and just sat there, glowing a beautiful golden color. Beverly decided that it must be a huge lightning bug, so she got closer to the window. Startled, the light swam away with the same movements an underwater creature would use until it disappeared into another dimension.

Beverly says, "That's when I knew I'd seen a fairy! I often think back to this experience with great joy and gratitude. In my heart, I

know that I have a fairy friend." Now Beverly
and her three-year-old daughter, Wendy, light
a candle and leave out bowls of milk and hon-
ey for fairies every night.

Ask the fairies to help you see them. Then stay
open to fairy lights and trust what you see. The lights
are a wonderful way to introduce your eyes to ob-
serving subtle forms of energy such as auras. As you
see fairy lights, you're developing spiritual muscles
so that you can see the fairies themselves with your
physical sight. This development also depends upon
your clearly deciding to see the fairies, without any
fears or doubts.

Angela Hartfield was able to see the fairies of Ireland when she became determined to do so:

Angela and her husband, Duke, both saw
fairies with their physical eyes while visiting
Glendalough park near Dublin, Ireland, in
2003. Irish natives had told the couple that if
the fairies wished to be seen, they'd become
visible. They also advised them to listen quietly for the fairies' music.

Although Angela had seen fairies in her mind's eye previously, she really wanted to see them with her physical eyes. So she set the intention on the way to Glendalough. In her heart, she knew that she'd get to see the fairies that day. After all, she'd been told that the park was a fairy sanctuary, filled with elementals.

As soon as they arrived at Glendalough, Angela could feel its mystical energy. An Irish friend named Fiona pointed and said, "Look at this bush. It's covered in fairies!" Angela could see dozens of fairies in her mind's eye, yet not as tangible beings.

So Angela again asked the fairies to reveal themselves to her. She kept getting the message to be patient while the fairies checked out her energy. So she relinquished her strong desire to see the fairies and just relaxed as she and Duke wandered through the park.

Duke was enjoying himself while gazing at the beauty around him. He said to Angela, "Do you see that dragonfly? I think that's the largest one I've ever seen! The body is such a strange color."

Angela looked in the direction where he was pointing and began to stare at this larger-than-usual dragonfly. She about jumped out of her skin in excitement and said, "Duke, that isn't a dragonfly. Look at the body. There are two legs right there. You just found the fairies!" She then looked beyond Duke's head and saw hundreds of them. They were so beautiful!

Angela says, "The fairies gave us the message that each of us comes upon our magic at the time most appropriate for us. We stood there watching these magical beings until other people came upon the area that we were standing in. Then the fairies quietly slipped back into their ethereal bodies. I could still see them in my mind's eye, but I'd been blessed with the gift of truly seeing them."

Photographs of Fairies

Another way to see fairies is by taking photographs outdoors in nature. As you take the photos, ask the fairies to reveal themselves. Many people have shown me photographs of orbs of light hovering in fields.

These are the fairy lights captured in photographs.

Sometimes the actual image of the elemental appears in the photograph as well. Usually, the photographer doesn't see these lights or images through the camera viewfinder. It's only after the picture is taken that the elementals are apparent in the photos.

Reverend Pomaika'i Coulon of Kapa'au, Hawaii, found a *menehune* (a Hawaiian elemental) in a photograph she'd taken following a nature spirit offering:

Pomaika'i felt blessed for all that she'd received from the spirits of Hawaii. She wanted to give something back to the land that had nurtured her through a healing process, so she decided to leave an offering on the land for the menehune, the spirits known as the "little people," who were the original inhabitants of the islands. Her gift to them would be an *ipu heke,* a double gourd drum that she'd made with weeks of labor and love.

On the day of the offering, Pomaika'i walked down a hillside to the stream that runs through her property and stopped at an old Hawaiian homestead. To her right was a very large grove of banyan trees. As Pomaika'i approached the trees, she noticed that they grew in a circle. She walked through an opening in the circle and began chanting and praying. She turned around and saw another, smaller circle of trees to her left.

Pomaika'i entered this circle, knowing immediately that this was where she'd leave her offering. She placed her ipu with great love and slight sadness. She said some more chants and prayers, then said thanks and began to leave. Before she left, Pomaika'i took a photograph of her ipu.

She recalls, "As I looked at the photo in my viewfinder, I thought something was wrong with my camera, as the color looked like sepia instead of full-color. I checked the camera's settings, but they were all normal. So I took another photograph just to be sure I had a good one. I left the large circle of banyans and started to cross back over the stream when I looked at the second photograph. Pictures speak louder than words. Menehunes are real!"

Pomaika'i's offering of the ipu heke,
a gourd drum that she'd made herself.

A menehune accepts the offering.

The fairies and other elementals are making themselves known through photographs and visions. The fairies know that seeing is believing. Our belief in, and connection with, the fairies gives them strength and power. And the more power that the fairies have, the more they can heal and protect the environment and the animals.

That's good news for all of us.

10 Ways to Make the Fairies Happy

Unlike humans, the fairies are pretty uncomplicated beings. They want to peacefully coexist with people, so if you reach out to them, they'll reach back to you. Here are some things that are especially meaningful to fairies to show your desire to connect with them and help them with their global mission:

1. Keep bird feeders full of food and water in your yard.

2. Place unwrapped candy outdoors for the fairies to enjoy, especially chocolate.

3. Plant bell-shaped flowers in your garden.

4. Switch to Earth-friendly soap, shampoo, and cleaning supplies (available at any health-food store).

5. Eat a vegan diet, or only buy humanely treated animals and animal products from organic farms.

6. Donate time or money to environmental or animal-rights charities.

7. Put statues of fairies or gnomes in your garden.

8. Hang crystals from your trees, and put them, or other shiny objects, in your yard.

9. Warn the fairies before you mow the grass, don't use pesticides, and celebrate

when toadstools and mushrooms appear in your yard because that means the fairies have taken up residence in your garden.

10. Relax or play in your yard, especially with music in the background.

FREQUENTLY ASKED QUESTIONS ABOUT THE FAIRIES

*S*o many myths surround fairies and the other elementals that there are frequent misconceptions and confusion over who they are and how they act. Here are some of the questions that I'm often asked about the fairies, and the answers that I've received through my experiences and interactions with the elemental realm:

Q: Are fairies mischievous pranksters?

A: Fairies, like all humans and other Earth-dwellers, have egos. That means that they don't automatically love everyone unconditionally as the egoless angels do. Fairies are very loving beings, but they favor people who treat the environment and animals kindly.

Since fairies play tricks on those who mistreat nature or animals, they've earned a reputation for mischief. Fairies also love parties, playfulness, dancing, and music. As these behaviors have been frowned upon at various times in our societal and religious history, these beings have also been denigrated.

Q: Are fairies real, or are they mythical?

A: Fairies are as real as you and me. They're as real as angels. Yet, only people who believe, are open-minded, or have a pure heart can sense or see them. Fairies are very shy and sensitive beings who hide from harsh environments or people. So those who are prone to skepticism can't see or feel the fairies.

Cultures also have an influence on people's acceptance of the fairies. In the United Kingdom (especially Ireland and Scotland), Australia, Polynesia, and other countries, there's a widespread belief in fairies and elementals. The countries that treat nature and animals with the most respect also tend to have the highest belief in fairies.

Q: Where can I find fairies?

A: Fairies live wherever there are plants or animals. They live near houseplants and pets. However, they're especially fond of the wilderness. They don't like pesticides or tightly manicured gardens.

Q: A psychic told me that she saw fairies around me. What does that mean?

A: Some people have fairies as spirit guides. Fairies stay with people who have a life purpose involving environmentalism or animals. You can ask the fairies for guidance about how to help the earth. In addition, fairies help us lighten up and be playful.

Q: Are fairies fallen angels?

A: God made fairies as the angels of nature. They're beings of pure, Divine light and love with an important mission of healing and protecting the environment and animals. Like humans, fairies have egos. So they're not unconditionally loving like the celestial angels. However, fairies are kind and fair.

Q: Can you trust fairies? Do they ever harm people?

A: You earn the fairies' respect by extending kindness toward Mother Nature. Recycling, using Earth-friendly cleaning supplies (available at any health-food store), and donating to environmental causes are just a few of the behaviors that fairies look for in their potential human friends. Once you earn the fairies' respect, they'll do anything for you.

Fairies don't harm people, but they can play tricks on those whom they view as cruel toward animals or the environment. Sometimes they play mild practical jokes (like temporarily hiding things) on people they love as a way of being playful.

Q: Can fairies become human, or vice versa?

A: Some people who look like fairies, gnomes, leprechauns, mermaids, and pixies are elemental souls who've elected to have human lives so that they can help the environment and animals in a big way. I've written about this topic in my books *Healing with the Fairies, Earth Angels,* and *Goddesses & Angels.*

Q: Is it true that fairies or leprechauns can bring you a pot of gold?

A: Many people (including those in some of the stories in this book) report that the elementals help them with finances. While the fairies and leprechauns usually don't bring literal pots of gold, they do bestow good fortune upon those humans whom they favor. This is one of many reasons to make friends with the fairies.

ABOUT THE AUTHOR

Doreen Virtue is a fourth-generation metaphysician and the author of the *Healing with the Angels* and *Healing with the Fairies* books and oracle cards; *Archangels & Ascended Masters;* and *Angel Therapy,* among other works. Her products are available in most languages worldwide.

A lifelong clairvoyant who works with the angelic, elemental, and ascended-master realms, Doreen holds Ph.D., M.A., and B.A. university degrees in counseling psychology, and is a former director of inpatient and outpatient psychiatric facilities at various hospitals.

Doreen has appeared on *Oprah*, CNN, *The View*, and other television and radio programs. For more information on Doreen and the workshops she presents throughout the world, to subscribe to Doreen's free e-mail angel-messages newsletter, to visit her message boards, or to submit your angel healing stories, please visit **www.AngelTherapy.com**.

You can listen to Doreen's live weekly radio show and call her for a reading by visiting **HayHouse Radio.com**®.

ABOUT THE ARTIST

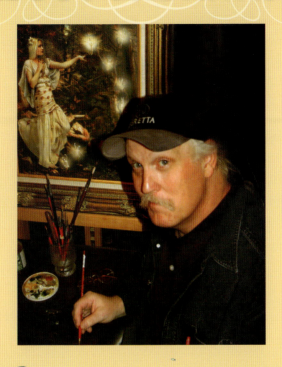

*H*oward David Johnson is a visual artist with a background in the natural sciences and history. He works in a wide variety of media ranging from traditional oils to digital media. After a lifetime of drawing and painting, his art was exhibited in the British Museum in London in 1996, as well as many others, including the Metropolitan Museum of Art. His work has appeared in every major bookstore in America as well as magazines and educational texts around the world. As an illustrator, he has not only used the computer but has been involved in developing and marketing software for Adobe Photoshop.

Please visit him at **www.howarddavidjohnson. com.**

Notes

Hay House Titles of Related Interest

ANIMALS AND THE AFTERLIFE:
True Stories of Our Best Friends' Journey Beyond Death,
by Kim Sheridan

ANIMAL SPIRIT GUIDES:
An Easy-to-Use Handbook for Identifying and Understanding Your Power Animals and Animal Spirit Helpers,
by Steven D. Farmer, Ph.D.

COMMUNICATION WITH ALL LIFE:
Revelations of an Animal Communicator, by Joan Ranquet

LOVE THYSELF:
The Message from Water III, by Masaru Emoto

POWER ANIMALS:
How to Connect with Your Animal Spirit Guides
(a book-with-CD), by Steven D. Farmer, Ph.D.

All of the above are available at your local bookstore,
or may be ordered by contacting Hay House
(see next page).

We hope you enjoyed this Hay House Lifestyles book.
If you'd like to receive our online catalog featuring additional information on Hay House books and products, or if you'd like to find out more about the Hay Foundation, please contact:

Hay House, Inc.
P.O. Box 5100
Carlsbad, CA 92018-5100

(760) 431-7695 or (800) 654-5126
(760) 431-6948 (fax) or (800) 650-5115 (fax)
www.hayhouse.com® • www.hayfoundation.org

Published and distributed in Australia by:
Hay House Australia Pty. Ltd., 18/36 Ralph St., Alexandria NSW 2015
Phone: 612-9669-4299 • *Fax:* 612-9669-4144 • www.hayhouse.com.au

Published and distributed in the United Kingdom by:
Hay House UK, Ltd., 292B Kensal Rd., London W10 5BE • *Phone:*
44-20-8962-1230 • Fax: 44-20-8962-1239 • www.hayhouse.co.uk

Published and distributed in the Republic of South Africa by:
Hay House SA (Pty), Ltd., P.O. Box 990, Witkoppen 2068
Phone/Fax: 27-11-467-8904 • www.hayhouse.co.za

Published in India by: Hay House Publishers India,
Muskaan Complex, Plot No. 3, B-2, Vasant Kunj, New Delhi 110 070
Phone: 91-11-4176-1620 • *Fax:* 91-11-4176-1630 • www.hayhouse.co.in

Distributed in Canada by:
Raincoast, 9050 Shaughnessy St., Vancouver, B.C. V6P 6E5
Phone: (604) 323-7100 • *Fax:* (604) 323-2600 • www.raincoast.com

Take Your Soul on a Vacation

Visit **www.HealYourLife.com®** to regroup, recharge, and reconnect
with your own magnificence.Featuring blogs, mind-body-spirit news,
and life-changing wisdom from Louise Hay and friends.

Visit **www.HealYourLife.com** today